DEVSECOPS WITH JENKINS

Creating a continuous delivery pipeline

Richard Lerbirato

ISBN-13: 9798842795352
ISBN-10: 1477123456

Cover design by: Art Painter
Library of Congress Control Number: 2018675309
Printed in the United States of America

INTRODUCTION

This book seeks to introduce the reader to the DevOps pattern, evolving to DevSecOps.

It will then be taught and exemplified how to build a DevSecOps pipeline using the Jenkins tool for continuous delivery (CI/CD)."

We'll also use SonarQube, learn about unit testing, functional testing, and API testing, and put all of this to work automatically.

You will only commit your code and the pipeline will build, test, deploy and even test the user interface!

At the end, you'll be able to mount a complete DevSecOps pipeline, automating the deploy and testing of your application, including simulation of clicks and insertions in the browser.

It is an indispensable read for IT infrastructure developers and architects.

DEVOPS

The DEVOPS standard has revolutionized application development and IT lifecycle maintenance. The watchwords are: Agility and Efficiency.

Before, we had separate teams: The development team was disasided with the infrastructure at the time of raising the code to the server and the team that took care of the environment felt chills when the development team informed the development of a new version of the software.

DevOps unific development and has automated development, from coding to deploying new versions.

The idea of DevOps is that there is quick feedback, a fast incident handling and especially a more accurate version delivery.

If you don't know, the ideal DevOps architecture indicates that the developer will launch your code into a repository, and from there an entire pipeline will automatically be created that will pick up this code, compile, perform performance checks, and then deploy.

All this without human interference. Only by performing once the build, analysis settings (memory usage, cpu, etc.) and the system send settings to your definitive environment, whether development, homologation, or production.

To set up this pipeline, teams must come together, master the system, and then agree on the appropriate parameters at each stage.

Such a methodology has clearly brought numerous benefits, but there is still a bottleneck to be corrected: Safety.

Most applications end up going to the production environment without protecting the most current vulnerabilities for development time issues.

Imagine the situation: You need to deliver a module of a system and your deadline is running out. Will you devote yourself to performing the final tests, repeating them, or will you research the latest security holes to see if your code is immune to them?

Of course the team won't spend their precious time for the final tests on safety, will they? That's exactly where the flaw is and that's the reason for so many cyber intrusions that we have in the present day.

For this, the concept of DevOps has evolved into DevSecOps.

Consider as if it were a more current version of DevOps, so it's DevSecOps you have to master.

DEV SEC OPS
DevOps vs. DevSecOps

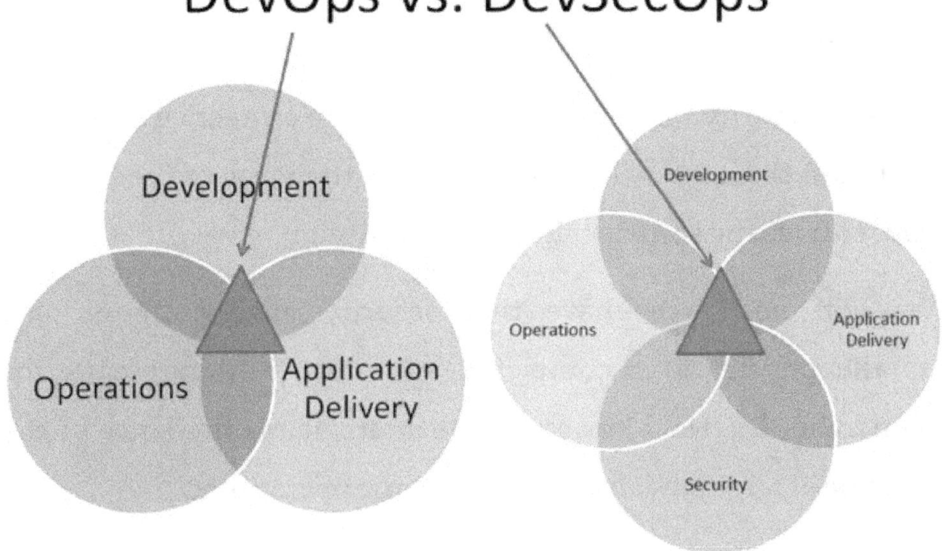

Literally, DEV-SEC-OPS indicates Development, Security, and Operations.

It is a standard of culture and platform structure that aims to give these characteristics to the life cycle of information technology.

Notice that we are not just talking about development. Always keep in mind that the methodology includes security, so the teams involved in these protections must be integrated into DevSecOps.

It is necessary to understand that this evolution of DEVOPS involves not only the addition of a security team to monitor the application, but that security should be present throughout the cycle, in a permanent and mainly automated way.

A security automation plan must be created so that developers are aware of the most contemporary threats when generating and maintaining code.

You see, security in DevSecOps is not a mere protective cover that is around the application, but rather all the steps of the pipeline have to have the security element in its design.

We will no longer have that security analyst figure pick up the project after completed and start running scans for vulnerabilities. Now he acts in the strategic maintenance of the pipeline at all stages and no longer in the operational.

Even this concept we call ShiftLeft, that is, we anticipate security care to prevent failures.

To help with this, it is recommended to appoint a Security Champion, who would be a professional or group of professionals with development and security knowledge.

The idea is that this Security Champion has the ability to be a promoter of communication and translation between the development team and the security team.

PIPELINES DE CI/CD/CS

The acronym is almost self-explanatory: Continuous Integration and Continuous Delivery.

In Portuguese, Continuous Integration and Delivery.

Continuous Security was added , completing the concept in its latest version.

We then have that this is a pipeline where several predefined steps will ensure that the delivery of software versions will follow the indications of DevSecOps, including monitoring.

In case we get the most gain, we're going to need this process to be automated.

Usually, a CI-CD pipeline is made up of the Build, Test, Release, Deployment, and Validation steps.

But each development company will have its own organization of steps that better satisfy the specific flow of the corporation.

CI-CD can be implemented on both virtual machines and container architecture, generating a pipeline for software delivery.

There is also an OpenSource project titled Tekton available for implementing this pipeline for cloud-native microservices.

This project even allows integration with other pipeline tools such as Skaffold, Knative, and Jenkins.

WORKING DEVOPS (DEVSECOPS) IN PRACTICE

Most of the literature on DevOps and DevSecOps doesn't take a practical example so that the professional can get a good look at what we're talking about.

Therefore, we will take a brief pause to give this insight that will help, and a lot, in understanding the concept.

As we speak, the idea of DevOps (and DevSecOps) is the continuous integration between development, operation, and security assumptions.

Besides, we want this automated.

Hence we created the CI/CD pipeline.

In this wake, the first iteration will be the availability (or alteration) of the application source code.

In fact, this will be the only human action! The goal of the pipeline is that the other steps are all automated.

The developer will commit your code, and this code will circulate across the pipeline through various checks until it reaches the build.

For example, we have several verifications that make sure the quality of the code before you build. Repeated classes, inefficient code, among others.

Then, it will continue the pipeline until the application is dedeployed.

After the build and before deploy, we have new testers on the pipeline that will analyze for example if there is excessive garbage production in java code, among other performance assumptions.

The pipeline will be previously configured in conjunction with the infrastructure and operations team.

Right, but in the company there are 3 teams that develop in different programming languages.

No problem, as many pipelines will be configured as needed.

If it is a Java application, the build is in a way. If it is a PHP application, it will be otherwise.

In the same way when you reach the Deploy step of the pipeline. If it is Java application it will follow the Java pipeline and deploy it will be on a server that supports jboss.

If it is PHP, the pipeline will take care of allocating the application to a web server such as Apache.

The developer doesn't have to worry about the infrastructure when committing their code because they've already sat down with that team in the pipeline assembly and have already passed on their needs to them.

Very good. But what about the evolution of DevSecOps? Where's the built-in security?

At every step!

In the steps before the build, the code will be checked to identify flaws that can leave gaps for attackers.

Also, before the build, a step can be placed where the pipeline checks the project dependencies to identify whether packages already defined by the team as unsafe or that have known security holes are being used.

After the build can be added testers on the pipeline to reanalyze the safety of the application, in particular the socket openings, apis availables.

See that it would be difficult to make a meeting for each change in the project just to discuss all these steps.

With this automated pipeline, the programmer will lift a code change, and the pipeline will already inform you that that dependency used has a security flaw, or you will warn that your code has a routine that consumes excessive memory.

It is indeed a powerful integration that generates quality to the software.

POST MORTEM MEETING

In IT, a post-mortem meeting and report is that feedback after a project is finalised or an incident is resolved.

The idea is that bringing together the teams of Dev, Sec and Ops, self-criticism and inquiries are carried out so that the next project does not repeat the same failures and that already act with the positive returns that the meeting will generate.

So, the purpose of this meeting is: to improve the way of acting as a team.

You don't try to find guilty or simply name faults. The goal is that together they find solutions to the new challenges to come, and of course, perpetuate the successful steps that have just ended.

THERE IS NO PERFECT SECURITY

That's right, i'm going to get It doesn't exist.

Whenever there is human interaction, there will be the possibility of failure. And we saw that the pipeline is developed by humans.

The team should consider the risk-return of their solutions and loopholes.

If the possibility of an event occurring is remote, the business impact in the event of a claim is low, but to implement valid security you need to sacrifice months of development or sacrifice the performance of the application , why implement it?

Of course, such a decision already requires approval from members of the business strategy, and it cannot be restricted to IT assuming such responsibility.

IT provides the information to the business manager and it assesses whether the risk is valid near the damage of protecting it more effectively.

CONTINUOUS AND ADAPTIVE RISK AND TRUST ANALYSIS

Created by Gartner, it's an architecture where IT security decisions must continually adapt.

Provides 3 phases: Run, Build and Plan.

In execution, data analysis is performed through Big Data and Machine Learning. The goal is to reduce the time to detect attacks.

For construction, it is necessary to evaluate all the company's documentation. Policies, infrastructure, data.

The construction is done in 4 steps:

- The first involves risk prevention, anticipating threats.
- Then one should isolate the system by hardening rules.
- Then, monitoring the entire IT of the company, identifying events.
- And then take the measures to sanitation the events.

For planning, data such as frequency of attacks, criticality of exposed data, among others, will be collected.

The aim is to avoid spending a large amount of financial resources to protect a risk that has little impact if exploited.

See that in any case, CARTA will already bring a benefit to be used by the company: The use of the data collected in the analysis.

But for the model to work fully, alignment between company management and the data security team is critical.

DEPLOY ON DEVOPS

We have some major types of deploy in Devops and your choice varies according to the personal possibilities of each available project and infrastructure.

Rolling

First we have Deploy Rolling. This way involves loading the services into a new version and then replacing the old version of the service.

In other words, it is a gradual process, not a drastic change. Consequently, the old version is only disabled when the new version is 100% functional. The switch or key turn will then take place.

The problem with this form of deploy is the need to administer two simultaneous versions until the change is fully completed.

Imagine two versions of the application in the air and writing in the same database.

Bluegreen

The Bluegreen deploy method works similar to Rolling, but a copy of the environment will be generated and a load balancer is placed to orchestrate the environments.

Then, you'll define that your tests will be performed in your environment without users losing access to the active application.

Of course, we see the disadvantage of doubling the whole environment.

Canary

In the Canary method there is the availability of a "beta" version for a small group of testers. The active application is still running and available to the general public.

It is an excellent way to test the application without compromising the user.

At the same time, you have user feedback regarding your experience. The problem is that this will take much more time and cost.

GAPS IN DEVSECOPS

A DevSecOps Pipeline already implemented has several steps.

Already the ideal pipeline would be one in which all phases are performed using good practices of DevSecOps.

With that, we'll have two mappings.

The current pipeline will be called "AS IS", while the ideal pipeline will be the "TO BE".

We will then have the confrontation between an array "AS IS" and a matrix "TO BE".

The differences between these two matrices will be called GAPS. We'll have an array of GAPS.

So, GAP is a nonconformity of some step of the pipeline in relation to the ideal according to the DevSecOps methodology.

We will assign a weight to each GAP according to the impact that its implementation generates.

A maturity matrix can also be created. This matrix would befed by the adjustments to be made in the GAPS matrix and the weight of each GAP, marking each as they are implemented, characterizing the evolution of the pipeline towards the ideal (TO BE Matrix).

TOOLS FOR AN EXAMPLE PIPELINE

There are several tools with which we can structure a DevSecOps pipeline accordingly.

Remember that we can separate in 4 steps:

Coding - Build - Tests and Migration - Deploy

For encoding, that is, for the software responsible for doing the control of source code versions, we can use Git, Sonatype Nexus, BitBucket, among others.

Their responsibility you already know. The Developer will commit and push your code to any of these repositories. That's the only entrance he gives to the pipeline.

From there, its code will follow through the steps automatically.

Then we'll have the next step, which is build.

To do this, specific tools such as Apache Maven will be activated, which builds applications in Java, PHP and others.

Docker can also be used to perform image build.

After the build, this result will be sent to the phase of the testes, and are several tools for different concepts.

We have SonarQube that evaluates static code, tracking potential bugs, resource waste, among other fixes to help the developer develop clean code.

We have Owasp Dependency Check toget known vulnerabilities into any of the dependencies used by the code after the build.

Also Junit, a tool for testing java code running on a JVM.

For the Deploy step, you can choose the desired platform, such as the OpenShift Containers platform.

AND WHO MANAGES THE PIPELINE?

Okay, you've already identified the phases of the pipeline, and the possible tools to be used.

But. Who performs the momentum and management of the steps?

Let's learn now.

JENKINS

Jenkins is the tool we use to seamlessly integrate.

It is he who will check for new versions of the source code, trigger the code analysis, trigger the build, deploy, that is, it is he who will coordinate the Pipeline.

You can download it for free https://jenkins.io

It is done in Java, so you will download a jenkins.war file and then run it by the command:

java -jar jenkins.war --httpPort=port-desired

It will perform the jenkins installation on the port you set.

After installation, the following screen will appear:

Create First Admin User

Username:

Password:

Confirm password:

Full name:

E-mail address:

You can then configure the address settings for this Jenkins instance:

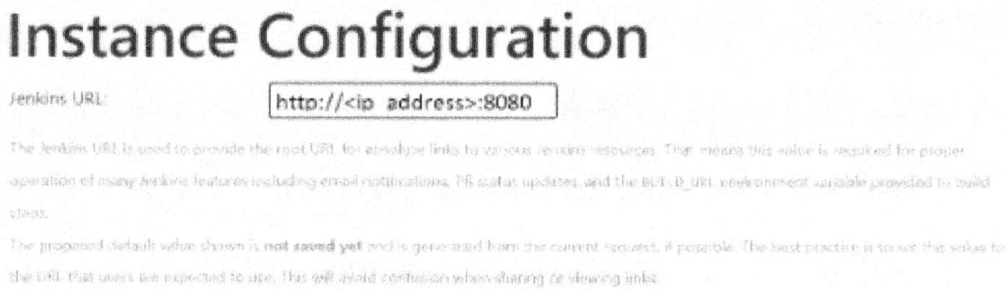

Instance Configuration

Jenkins URL: `http://<ip_address>:8080`

The Jenkins URL is used to provide the root URL for absolute links to various Jenkins resources. That means this value is required for proper operation of many Jenkins features including email notifications, PR status updates, and the BUILD_URL environment variable provided to build steps.

The proposed default value shown is not saved yet and is generated from the current request, if possible. The best practice is to set this value to the URL that users are expected to use. This will avoid confusion when sharing or viewing links.

Ready. It's as simple as that. Your Jenkins is installed.

You must now configure the Pipeline.

GLOBAL CONFIGURATION TOOL

Jenkins does not compile, Jenkins does not deploy. He actually invokes the tools that will do this.

Within the menu called Global Tool Configuration, we have:

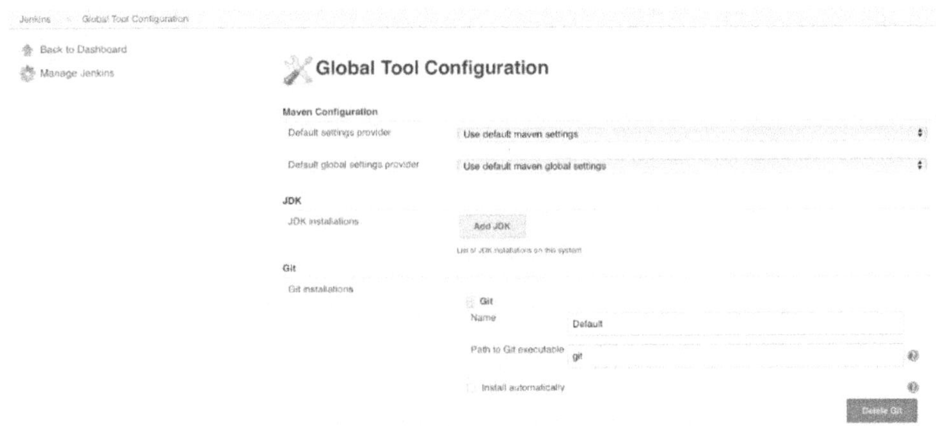

Here you will configure your JDK to run the jenkins tools.

An example of a tool settings menu:

Jenkins Location

Serve resource files from another domain

Propriedades globais

SonarQube servers

Pipeline Speed/Durability Settings

Usage Statistics

Test Management for Jira

Bitbucket Endpoints

Audit Trail

JIRA

Timestamper

Fingerprints

Administrative monitors configuration

Global Build Discarders

Lockable Resources Manager

GitHub

GitHub Enterprise Servers

Pipeline Model Definition

Master->Slave HTTP Proxy Service

In this example of the image above you can already view the Jenkins orchestration dimension.

JOBS DO JENKINS

The pipeline is a set of Jobs.

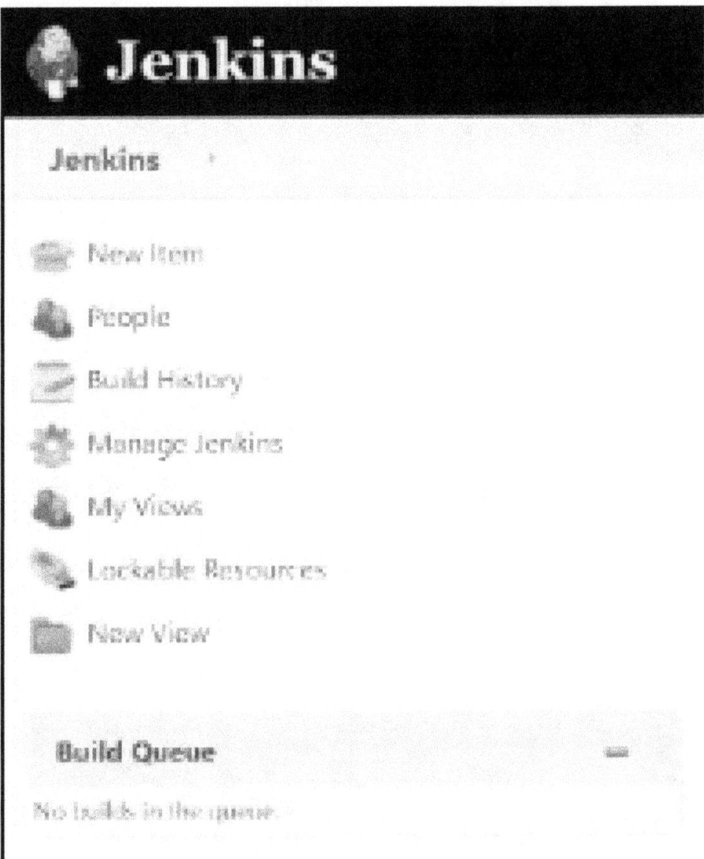

When you click the "New Item" menu, Jenkins will ask you what type of task you want to create:

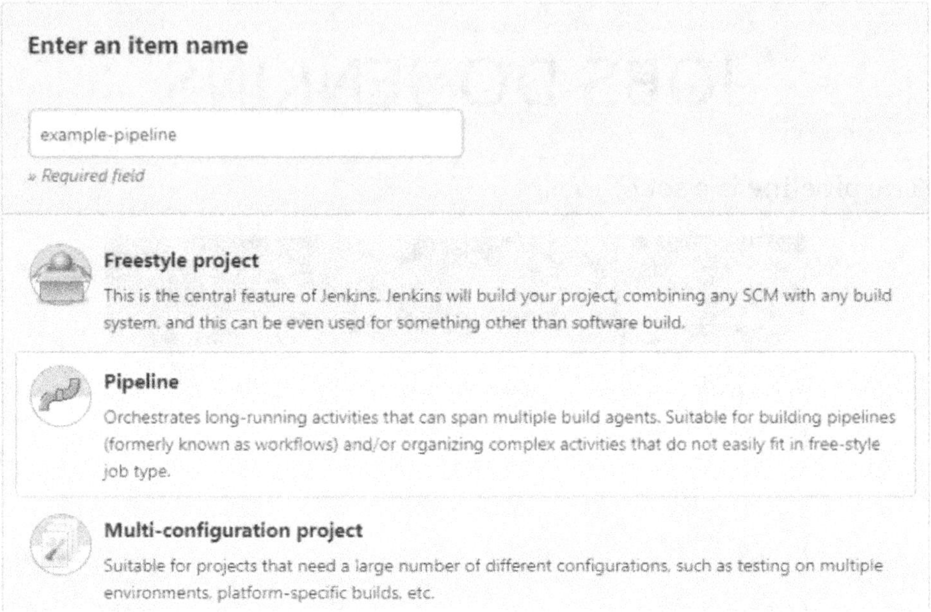

Enter an item name

example-pipeline

» Required field

Freestyle project

This is the central feature of Jenkins. Jenkins will build your project, combining any SCM with any build system, and this can be even used for something other than software build.

Pipeline

Orchestrates long-running activities that can span multiple build agents. Suitable for building pipelines (formerly known as workflows) and/or organizing complex activities that do not easily fit in free-style job type.

Multi-configuration project

Suitable for projects that need a large number of different configurations, such as testing on multiple environments, platform-specific builds, etc.

With the FreeStyle option your design will be very flexible.

But our idea here is to show the CI/CD pipeline, i.e. the DevOps Pipeline (DevSecOps).

SOURCE CODE

First step of the pipeline when it is in operation will always be the arrival of the source code.

The developer will put the source code in the Source Code Manager (SCM) that we set up with Jenkins.

For instance:

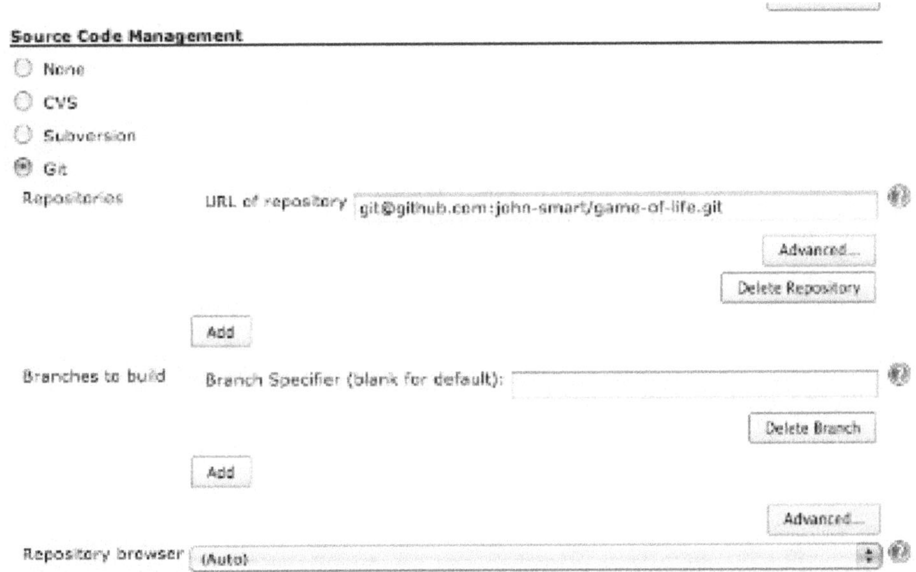

The pipeline begins with the application code being allocated in the SCM, so you must define one or more repositories before Jenkins can see it.

You will enter the read credentials for this version control so that Jenkins can trigger the pull of the code to send to the build step.

AUTOMATIC BUILD

Jenkins allows us to perform a manual build at the click of a button.

But that's not what you're aiming at using an orchestrator like Jenkins.

Remember that we are talking about a CI/CD pipeline within DevSecOps.

That is, we have a Continuous Integration (CI) and a Continuous Delivery (CD).

So, to be continuous according to DevOps (DevSecOps), we want the pipeline to be automated.

And that's what Jenkins allows us to:

Build Triggers

☑ Build whenever a SNAPSHOT dependency is built

☐ Schedule build when some upstream has no successful builds

☐ Trigger builds remotely (e.g. from scripts)

☐ Build GitHub Pull Requests

☐ Build after other projects are built

☐ Build periodically

☐ Experimental: GitHub Branches

☐ GitHub hook trigger for GITScm polling

☑ Poll SCM

Schedule   */1 * * * *

We can activate the build through remote scripts (which will be scheduled on some server such as using CronTab.

We also have the option to perform automatic build on a project as soon as another project is assembled.

And interestingly, we can define a periodicity for the application to be built.

So we can configure that every 5 minutes Jenkins will track the SCM for changes in the source code (git example) and then promote the build.

Note that Schedule uses the same format as Cron.

Therefore, we can follow the table in Cron's own manual, as

shown in the following image:

```
 ┌───────────── minute (0 - 59)
 │ ┌───────────── hour (0 - 23)
 │ │ ┌───────────── day of month (1 - 31)
 │ │ │ ┌───────────── month (1 - 12)
 │ │ │ │ ┌───────────── day of week (0 - 6) (Sunday to Saturday;
 │ │ │ │ │                                  7 is also Sunday on some systems)
 │ │ │ │ │
 │ │ │ │ │
 * * * * *  schedule command to execute
```

You can even place more than one schedule.

Jenkins allows the use of some aliases for more common periodicities:

So instead of using the ***** format you can use @hourly, @daily, @weekly, @monthly, @midnight.

For example, to build every midnight and weekly on Fridays at 5:30 pm, we will use two lines:

@midnight
30 17 * * 5

And of course, the ultimate in integration continuity is to perform automatic updates to version control in search of changes to the source code.

That is, the idea is that the develop commit and push your code to the SCM and from there he feels and watches Jenkins work, without even having to start the pipeline.

Everything will be automatically done by Jenkins.

Your tool can be a GIT implementation like BitBucket, or Subversion, or one another via script. All you have to do is teach the coordinates and Jenkins will do it for you!

Sure. Got the source code, let's see the build.

MAVEN

Build is run by a builder and not by Jenkins.

Jenkins is an orchestrator. It invokes the tools every step of the pipeline.

An example builder for the Java language is Apache Maven.

You can install it if your copy of Jenkins didn't come with the pre-configured integration.

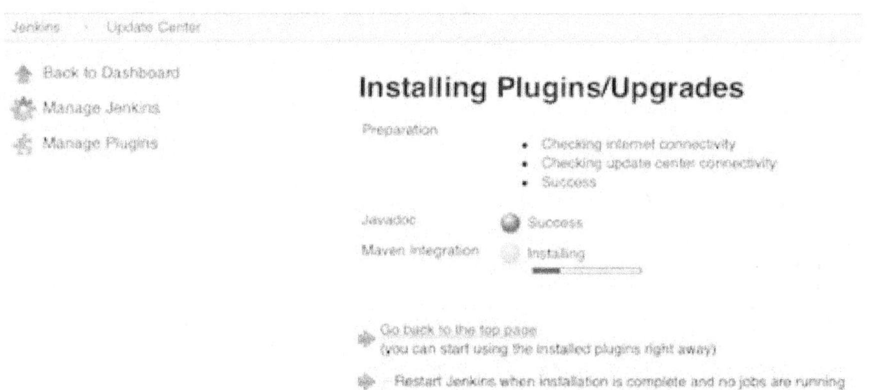

Installed the plugin, you will now have the possibility to use Maven for the build.

The settings for Maven vary from version to version, but are generally as simple as all Jenkins orchestration.

To use it, the developer will create a pom.xml file at the root of your source code and it is this file that will contain the settings for building and assembling the application.

If you don't create pom.xml, your console in jenkins will display:

```
Console output
Started by user anonymous
Building in workspace /Users/stephenc/src/plugins/console-tail-
plugin/work/workspace/foo
[foo] $ mvn clean verify
[INFO] Scanning for projects...
[INFO] ------------------------------------------------------------------------
[INFO] BUILD FAILURE
[INFO] ------------------------------------------------------------------------
[INFO] Total time: 0.112s
[INFO] Finished at: Tue Oct 22 14:07:53 IST 2013
[INFO] Final Memory: 2M/81M
[INFO] ------------------------------------------------------------------------
[ERROR] The goal you specified requires a project to execute but there is no POM in
this directory (/Users/stephenc/src/plugins/console-tail-plugin/work/workspace/foo).
Please verify you invoked Maven from the correct directory. -> [Help 1]
[ERROR]
[ERROR] To see the full stack trace of the errors, re-run Maven with the -e switch.
[ERROR] Re-run Maven using the -X switch to enable full debug logging.
[ERROR]
[ERROR] For more information about the errors and possible solutions, please read the
following articles:
[ERROR] [Help 1]
http://cwiki.apache.org/confluence/display/MAVEN/MissingProjectException
Build step 'Invoke top-level Maven targets' marked build as failure
Finished: FAILURE
```

There is even the possibility for Jenkins to create a pipeline from data contained in the pom.xml file, making the life of the orchestrator easier.

DEPLOY

To perform the deploy we will also install plugins.

There are already a few available in the installation.

The idea is that in the Pipeline you go and click the button: Add Post-Build Action:

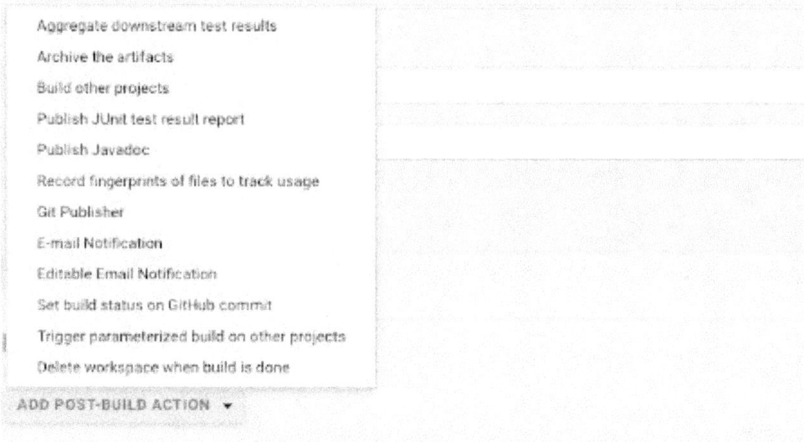

A list will appear as above according to the plugins you have installed.

For example, if you want to deploy to a Containers platform using Kubernetes, you can install the plugin: Deploy to Container Plugin

Install ↓	Name	Version
☐	**Artifact Deployer Plug-in** This plugin makes it possible to copy artifacts to remote locations.	0.33
☐	**AWS Lambda Plugin** This plugin adds AWS Lambda invocation and deployment abilities to build steps and post build actions	0.3.1
☐	**AWS Elastic Beanstalk Deployment Plugin** This plugin allows you to deploy into AWS Elastic Beanstalk by Packaging, Creating a new Application Version, and Updating an Environment	0.0.3
☐	**Capifornicat Plugin** This plugin deploy the WAR file to multiple remote Tomcat servers by using Capistrano 3	0.1.0
☐	**AWS CodeDeploy Plugin for Jenkins** Adds a post build step to integrate Jenkins with AWS CodeDeploy	1.7
☐	**CRX Content Package Deployer Plugin** Deploys content packages to Adobe CRX applications, like Adobe CQ 5.4, CQ 5.5, and AEM 6.x. Also allows downloading packages from one CRX server and uploading them to one or more other CRX servers	1.3.2
☑	**Deploy to container Plugin** This plugin takes a war/ear file and deploys that to a running remote application server at the end of a build	1.10
☐	**Deploy to Websphere container Plugin** This plugin is an extension of the Deploy Plugin. It takes a war/ear file and deploys that to a running remote WebSphere Application Server at the end of a build	1.0
☐	**XebiaLabs XL Deploy Plugin** The XL Deploy Plugin integrates Jenkins with XebiaLabs XL Deploy	5.0.0

Installed the plugin to deploy in Container, you can configure the post-build options by loading the product from the build step to be transported to a Container.

That is, it will appear in the Menu of Post-Build Actions, the option: Deploy to Container.

By adding this post-build step, you'll now set up:

Deploy war/ear to a container

WAR/EAR files	$WORKSPACE/cqnews-cms/target/cqnews-cms.war
Context path	cqnews-cms
Containers	Tomcat 8.x
	Credentials	tomcat/******	▾	← Add✦
	Tomcat URL	http://10.20.1.24:8081
	Add Container ▾
Deploy on failure	

Notice that we are using the Maven builder so of course our product will be a War/Ear.

First we point out the location to find the builder's output.

Context-Path is the name of the application.

Next, we select where the server is, which in our case will be TomCat 8.

We set up the credentials, and that's it.

These credentials are created by clicking the Add button, which will open the Jenkins Credentials Provider.

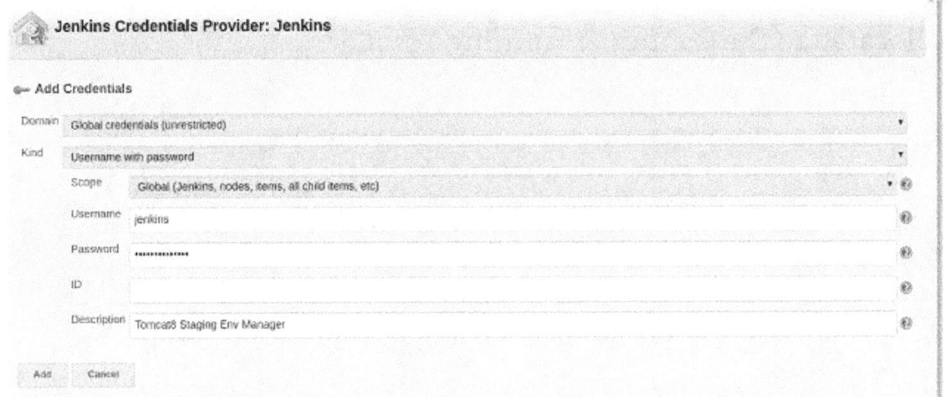

Ready. Click Build Now:

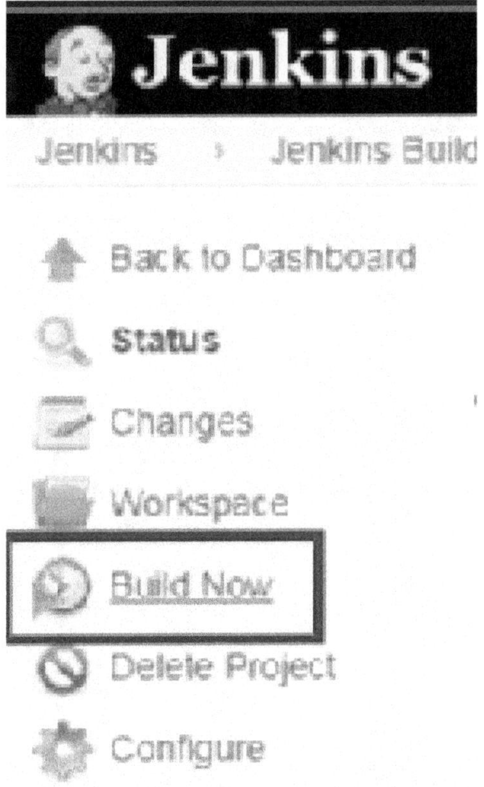

And you'll see the application being built and then already

allocated to the Container running TomCat.

BUILD TRIGGERS

As we've already said, you don't want to click build every time you commit and push your code.

For this, we have the configuration of the triggers:

Build Triggers

☑ Build whenever a SNAPSHOT dependency is built

☐ Schedule build when some upstream has no successful builds

☐ Trigger builds remotely (e.g. from scripts)

☐ Build GitHub Pull Requests

☐ Build after other projects are built

☐ Build periodically

☐ Experimental: GitHub Branches

☐ GitHub hook trigger for GITScm polling

☑ Poll SCM

Schedule   */1 * * * *

The most basic Trigger is the "Build Periodically" well similar to the CRON we saw in the previous section.

But that means taking down the server, performing the build, and restore it. That's right without changes. Whenever the time reaches the configured periodicity, there will be this process.

Therefore, even interesting is the use of SCM-Pool (Source Code Management), because this will not fire unnecessary builds.

From time to time, it will only check your source code control to identify changes and build if you find changes to the code.

The time setting for this period will also follow the CRON pattern.

HOOKS

Hooks are another way to fire builds.

Instead of Deploy-Job periodically asking GIT if there have been changes, we do the opposite.

Jenkins ' job is still, and git's going to let Jenkins know there's a change.

In the previous image with the Trigger options you can see an option, the GitHub Hook Trigger, already installed, although we have not selected it.

STATIC ANALYSIS

In static analysis we do not yet have the build.

We're checking the source code.

The analysis will look for variables that were used, but not declared, or variables that were not initialized.

In addition, it checks for excessive complexity in the code.

Within the development pipeline, the sooner you identify some coding flaw, the more economical the fix will be.

Static analysis has to provide speed, accuracy and depth in your scan.

The interesting thing is that this analysis will go through all possible paths of future execution of this code.

As we talked about in DevSecOps and no longer just in DevOps, it's interesting that the analysis of security already begins in this step as well.

You use the Qube Sonar tool for this.

SONARQUBE

SonarQube is the tool that will do our static analysis of the source codes within our jenkins pipeline.

You will install the SonarQube server, and then select and install the scanners based on your reality. There are dozens of languages that can be analyzed.

The platform allows for example the following scanners:

- Gradle - SonarScanner for Gradle
- .NET - SonarScanner for .NET
- Maven - use the SonarScanner for Maven
- Jenkins - SonarScanner for Jenkins
- Azure DevOps - SonarQube Extension for Azure DevOps
- Ant - SonarScanner for Ant
- anything else (CLI) - SonarScanner

If you are using the Community Edition version, you will only have access to the Scanner for Java and JS languages. To access other languages you must use a paid version.

INTEGRATING SONARQUBE WITH JENKINS

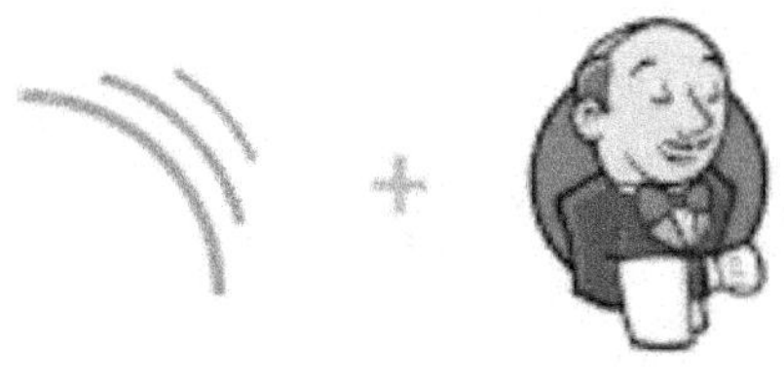

You will install SonarQube. Keep an eye out that it's pretty heavy, so evaluate whether it's worth climbing it on another machine or in Jenkins' own host.

After installation, it will be available at the address and port that you configured in the installation.

Once finished, you'll have access to an interface similar to this:

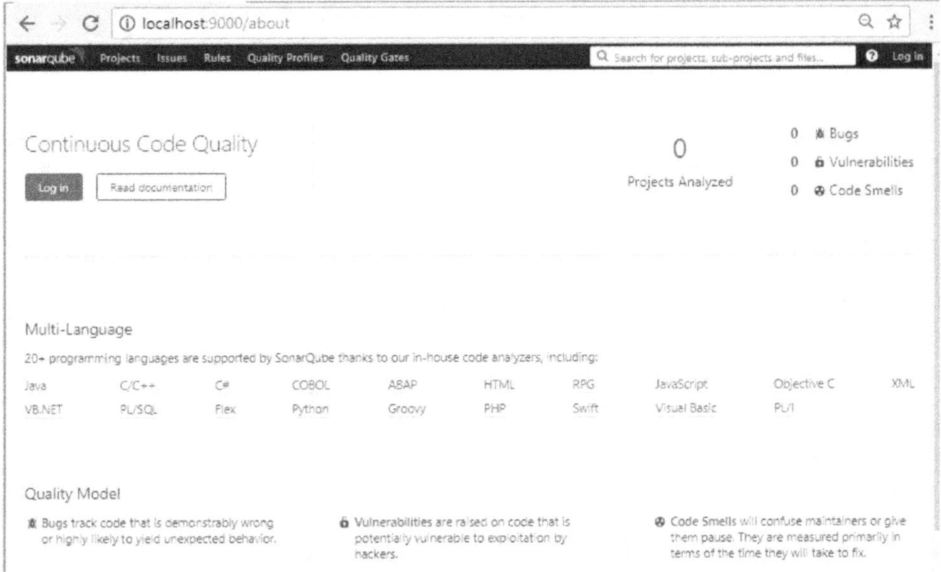

Perfect. Installed and available SonarQube, the first thing when integrating with Jenkins is to create a Token.

Go to the top right menu in My Account.

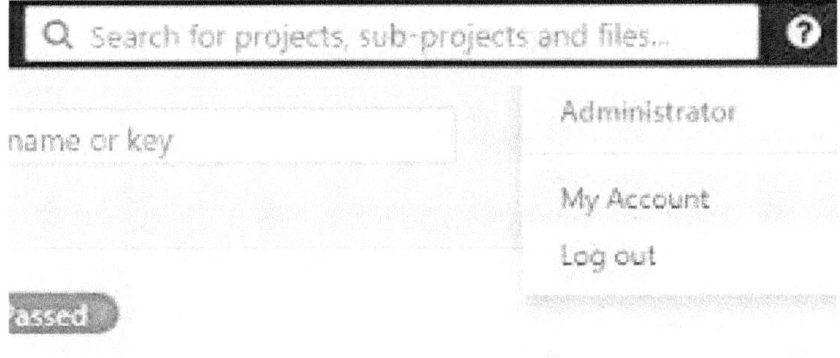

Then search for Security and the Generate Tokens option.

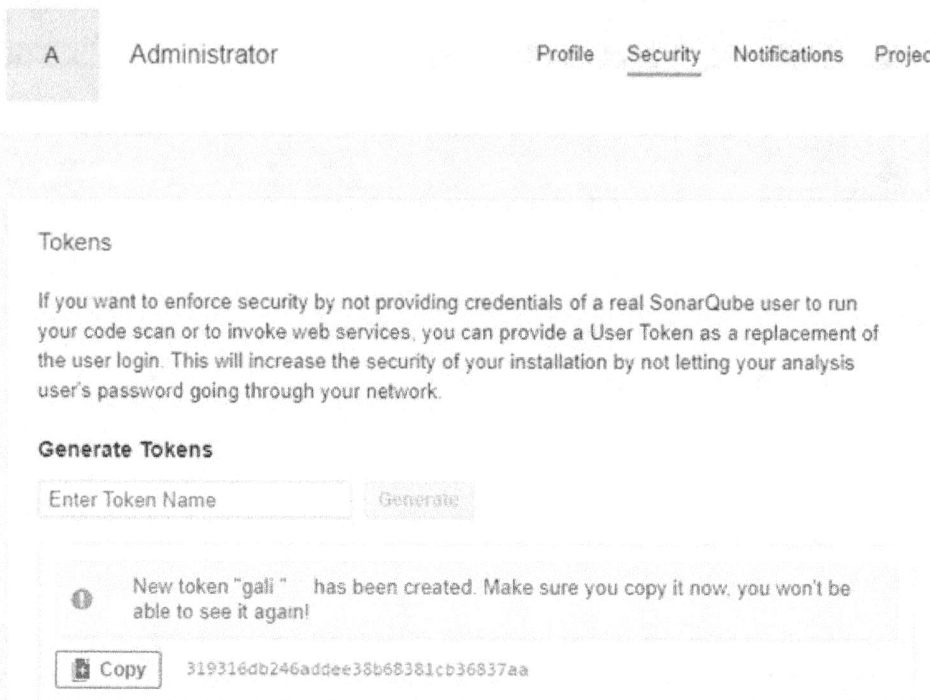

Here you will create a token so that Jenkins can access SonarQube.

Copy the token by clicking the Copy button.

Then go to Jenkins to install the Sonar plugin.

You will search for the SonarQube Scanner plugin.

Then you can go to Manage Jenkins and look for the new SonarQube section that came up when we installed the Plugin.

Choose the Secret Text Server Authentication Token and create a credential using the Token copied from SonarQube.

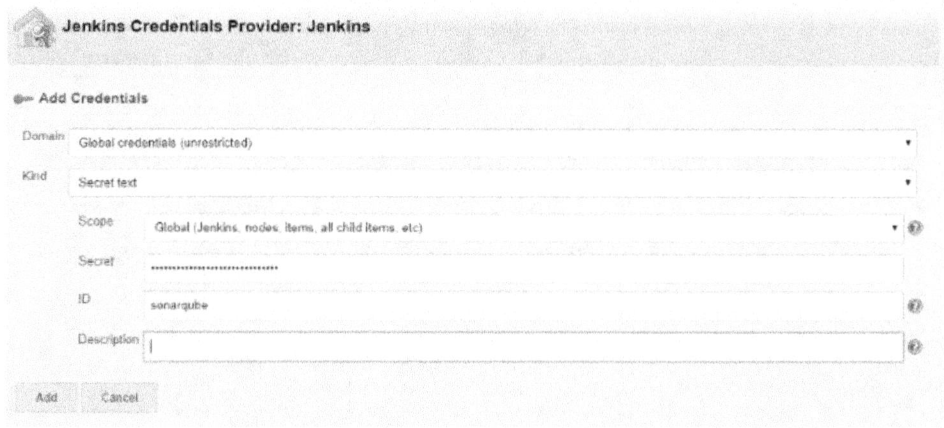

After you create, finish the configuration and SonarQube is integrated with Jenkins.

Now let's set up SonarQube's Quality Gate.

QUALITY GATE

Go to Jenkins and install the Sonar Quality Gates Plugin.

Then look for the new Quality Gates section near where you set up SonarQube in Jenkins.

Quality Gates - Sonarqube

Name	Sonar Server
	Make sure the name is unique value
SonarQube Server URL	http://sonarserver.local:8081
	Default value is 'http://localhost:9000'
SonarQube account token	
	Use token instead of user and password
SonarQube account login	admin
	Default value is 'admin'
SonarQube account password	••••••••••
	Default value is 'admin'
Maximum waiting time (milliseconds)	900000
	Default value is '300000' or 5 minutes
Time to wait next check (milliseconds)	60000
	Default value is '10000' or 10 seconds

Add Sonar instance

Enter the settings.

You can enter the Token instead of entering login and password.

In this case, you can leave the SonarQube account login and Sonar Qube account password blank.

Then go to Manage Jenkins, Global Tool, and click Add SonarQube Scanner.

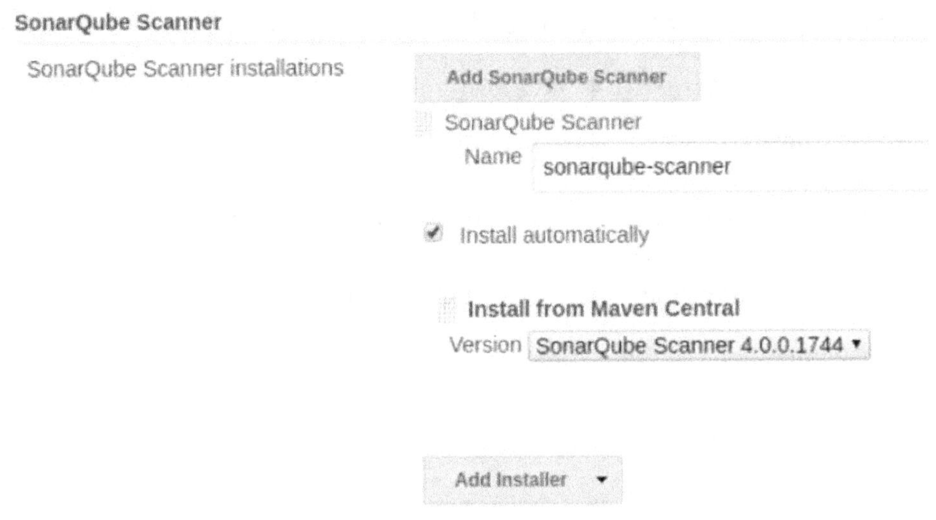

Sure. We set up Quality Gate, but what is this?

Quality Gates are species of minimum quality profiles that we have defined for the project to be considered approved by SonarQube.

That is, we can create a Quality Gate called: Strict.

And we define that for a project to be approved in this Quality Gate, it is necessary that it has no serious BUG, which has no more than 20 BUGS mediated, among other parameters that we can define.

In parallel we can create another quality gate with the name: Easy.

In this Quality Gate, we would define that for project approval, it would be enough that the analysis did not find more than 100 serious flaws.

That is, they are like a minimum quality score for the code.

Let's create a project at SonarQube and see the Quality Gates further down.

PROJECT AT SONARQUBE

Now that SonarQube is already fully integrated into Jenkins, we can create a project within it.

Go to SonarQube and click Create New Project.

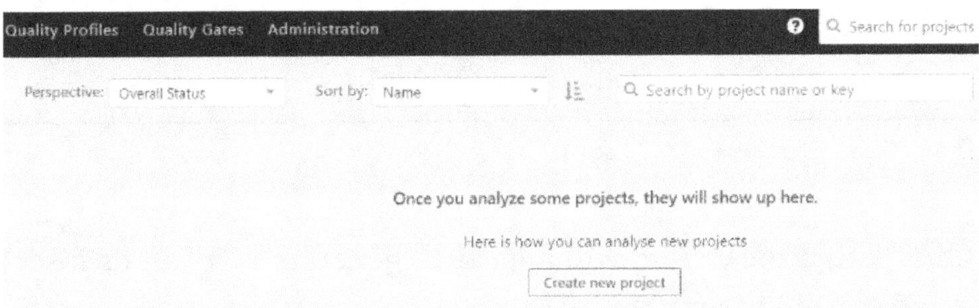

Enter the basic data:

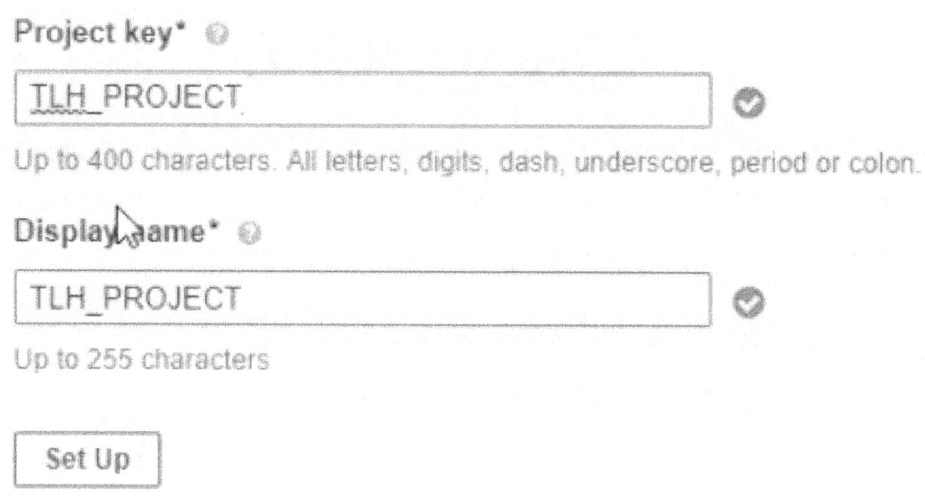

Click Setup, the screen will appear to generate a Token or insert the existing one.

Click generate a new one and continue.

Then select the language:

By selecting Java, the option will appear for you to choose the builder between Maven and Gradle.

Select Maven because that's what we're going to use, and give it ok.

SonarQube will provide on-screen codes to configure Jenkins, something like:

```
mvn sonar:sonar \
   -Dsonar.projectKey=demo-sonarqube \
   -Dsonar.host.url=http://localhost:9000 \
   -Dsonar.login=YOUR-TOKEN-HERE
```

You will copy only the bottom 3 lines. That is, copy only:

```
-Dsonar.projectKey=demo-sonarqube \
-Dsonar.host.url=http://localhost:9000 \
-Dsonar.login=YOUR-TOKEN-HERE
```

Leave this screen open or copy the code, and let's go back to Jenkins.

Let's add a step to the build:

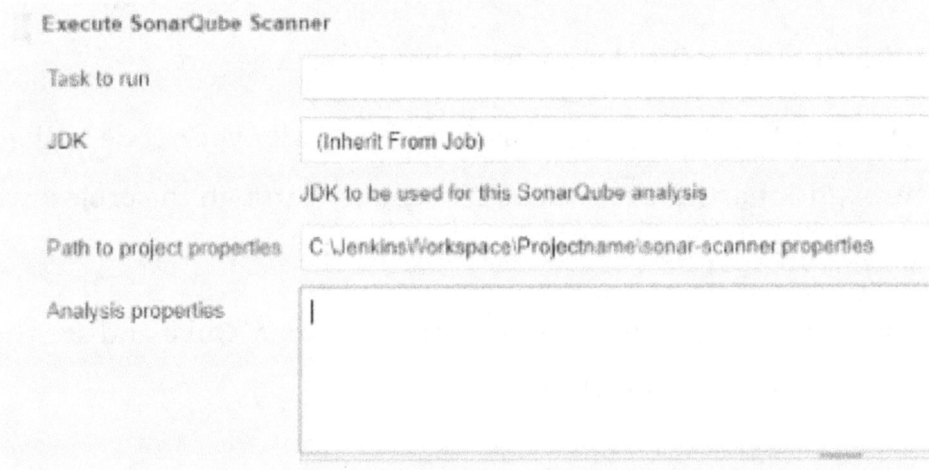

The screen will appear to set up the Scanner.

Leave everything blank except analysis properties, which you will fill with the last 3 lines you copied there from SonarQube in the previous step.

After copying, you must remove from the beginning of each line the "-D" parameter that is only for execution on the command line and remove the "\" at the end of the lines.

In our example the Analysis Properties field would look like this:

```
sonar.projectKey=demo-sonarqube
sonar.host.url=http://localhost:9000
sonar.login=YOUR-TOKEN-HERE
```

Of course, you will replace YOUR-TOKEN-HERE with your token.

Then add a fourth line with the following content:

```
sonar.java.binaries=target
```

With this you pointed out where the java binaries are.

Ready. Just perform a build and automatically your code will go through SonarQube to measure its quality through the project we connect.

Once the build is complete, you can go to SonarQube and see the Project analysis report there.

The result comes in the form of notes, being "A" the best grade and "E" the worst grade.

You are now seeing that the application has passed the test through the chosen Quality Gate.

He got a C for Bugs because he had 1 bug.

He got an A for Vulnerabilities since none were found.

Safely, he received a Grade E since six hot spots were found that could be exploited.

Well, if you got bad grades like that, how did you get through?

Simple. This Quality Gate is configured to approve projects (codes) that take a note in Security and at least note C in Bugs.

In fact, it's possibly the default Quality Gate tool, since we haven't created another one.

To change the Quality Gate of a Project, just go to the project administration menu:

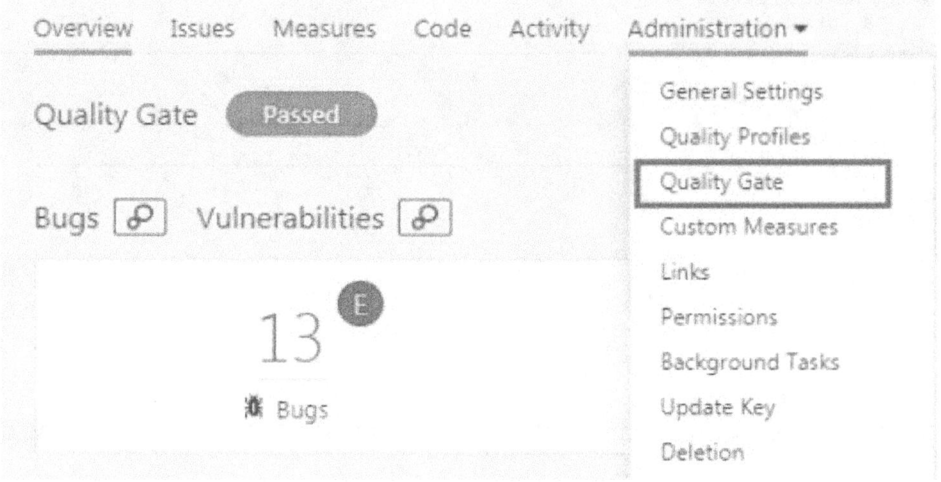

And then, choose Quality Gate to associate with the project:

Of course, you can and will create your custom Quality Gates, with the rules you find relevant to approving the codes in your environment.

In more critical security projects you will require a higher note in this issue in the quality gate, while in projects that require a lot of maintenance and future change it is customary to seek that the code is better done, with fewer code-smells.

But if you run the pipeline now, even if the analysis results in code disapproval when going through the Quality Gate that you defined for your SonarQube project, the code will be built and deployed anyway!

That's because we haven't yet defined how jenkins will use the response to this analysis.

To do this, we added a step in Post-Build:

Post-build Actions

Quality Gates Sonarqube Plugin

Sonar instance 'Name'   sonar-5

Choose sonar instance

Project Key   org.jenkins-ci.plugins:qa-plugin-sonar

Enter your project key.

Add post-build action

TECHNICAL DEBT

The great power of SonarQube is to show what the technical debt is.

See in the previous image.

We have the information:

$$4d\ 4h \quad \text{Debt}$$

That is, it takes 4 days and 4 hours for all the faults found to be corrected, in order to fix the BUG found, extinguish the 6 hotspots found, and so on.

The project passed this Quality Gate, but you might want to settle all these backlogs anyway. After all, the cleaner and more correct the code, the fewer future problems.

So you now already have a very good metric to send to the software factory and charge a quote for the refactoring of this code. Fantastic.

MAVEN ENFORCER

It is worth doing an ad to present a solution that integrates security in your DevOps, implementing what DevSecOps preaches, that is, that at all stages there is concern about security.

Before we go into the tests, let's look at an example plugin that seeks to update Maven to this pattern.

Maven Enforcer is designed to perform pre-build checks to ensure application security prior to compilation.

This is because often the build can be very time consuming, and it would be bad for the developer to wait too long to have information that for security reasons the build can not be performed.

After installing the Maven Enforcer plugin, it will be instantiated within the Pom.xml.

We will have a pom.xml with a structure similar to the following:

```xml
<plugins>
  <plugin>
    <groupId>org.apache.maven.plugins</groupId>
    <artifactId>maven-enforcer-plugin</artifactId>
    <version>3.1.0</version>
    <executions>
      <execution>
        <id>enforce-versions</id>
        <goals>
          <goal>enforce</goal>
        </goals>
        <configuration>
          <rules>
            <bannedPlugins>
              <!-- will only display a warning but does not fail the build. -->
              <level>WARN</level>
              <excludes>
                <exclude>org.apache.maven.plugins:maven-verifier-plugin</exclude>
              </excludes>
              <message>Please consider using the maven-invoker-plugin (http://maven.apache.org/plugins/maven-invoker-plugin/)!</message>
            </bannedPlugins>
            <requireMavenVersion>
              <version>2.0.6</version>
            </requireMavenVersion>
            <requireJavaVersion>
              <version>1.5</version>
            </requireJavaVersion>
            <requireOS>
              <family>unix</family>
            </requireOS>
          </rules>
        </configuration>
      </execution>
    </executions>
  </plugin>
</plugins>
```

There are several Built-In Rules in the plugin and you can even customize your rules.

For example, an interesting rule is that it verifies that any of the dependencies being linked by the application in the build have security flaws detected by the community.

You define whether to issue only one WARN, or an ERROR.

In the case of ERROR, the build will not run.

You can also ensure that the dependency store is not on a blacklist.

That is, it is a perfect DevSecOps plugin.

UNIT TEST IN JUNIT

Unit tests are fast. They are the most effective to be realized.

It is much easier to find an error within a unit test.

The developer will select in their application the classes and methods that are worth testing.

Not everyone does. For example, a class that only has one method with no calculation involved, without any manipulation of any variables, is irrelevant.

However, a business class, that is, that handles received data and returns a result, is prone to unit tests.

In addition, the test scenario is configured, that is, the possible entries that will be provided and the expected results.

For example, let's imagine a Java class that has only one method.

This method receives as parameter an integer, and the return of the method is false if the number is less than 4, and true if it is greater than or equal to 4.

So, let's draw up a test by passing as a parameter all possible integers?

Of course i'm not. That's impossible. We will use the so-called equivalence and limit value classes.

We will not be 100% sure that there will be no errors, but we have drastically reduced the chances of failure, and make testing possible.

In that case, we're going to pass a number greater than four, we're going to pass another number less than four, and we're going to pass number 4.

The numbers greater than 4 we say are in an equivalence class.

Numbers less than 4 will be in another equivalence class, and number 4 will be in a third equivalence class, in addition to being our limit value (between classes)."

Remember, we are using Java as a language and for build, Maven.

First we'll inform Maven of Junit's dependency.

We do this in the pom.xml:

```
<dependencies>
  <dependency>
    <groupId>junit</groupId>
    <artifactId>junit</artifactId>
    <version>3.8.1</version>
    <scope>test</scope>
  </dependency>
</dependencies>
```

Jacoco plugin is also installed to allow reporting and sending to SonarQube.

Then, in code, a test class is created within an src/test/java file.

Now, a file is created for the JUNIT tests.

Let's say our method was called Verify(INT N).

We will use junit's assert method to ensure code correction.

The junit test java file would look something like:

```java
Import org.junit.Assert;

Import org.junit.Test;

Public class JustATestRichardLerbirato

{

        @Test

        public void LetsTest

        {

                Assert.assertFalse(Verify(2));

                Assert.assertTrue(Verify(4));

                Assert.assertTrue(Verify(6));

        }

}
```

When you run the build, the 3 methods will be tested to make sure that the return is the long-awaited one, either True or False.

Of course, unit tests run away from the scope of our study here and so look at this chapter as just a hello-world of the testing world.

Advanced testing uses Mock, and we won't go into these details here.

This explanation was just for you to understand what unit tests are.

This is important because SonarQube has a quality parameter called Coverage, which is exactly how much of the code has test classes available.

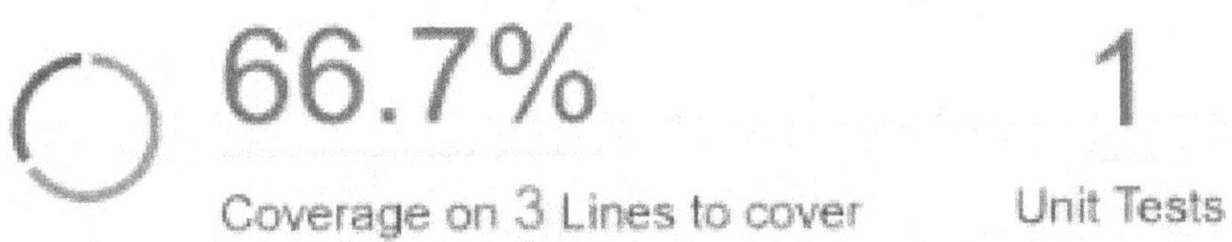

Applications that can't have crashes, such as banking, may have to go through a Quality Gate that has strict code coverage, say, above 90% for example.

The SonarQube report will display all classes and methods that have not been tested.

Sonar shows even if all conditions of a given method have been covered.

But ideally, we should tell SonarQube which packages it should require testing.

Otherwise, we would force the developer to create tests in unnecessary classes if we want 95% coverage for example.

To do this, you will add exclusions to coverage:

Code Coverage
Configure the files that should be ignored by code coverage calculations.

Coverage Exclusions
Patterns used to exclude some files from coverage report.
Key: sonar.coverage.exclusions

`**/vendor/**/*`

Reset   Default: <no value>

The same logic you will use for duplicate rows, and other checks.

This will greatly enhance your analysis with SonarQube.

In addition, you will gain in task processing speed.

REST API CHECKS

API stands for Application Programming Interface.

The idea is that your Front End doesn't communicate directly with the database.

Then, you will invoke an API, passing the parameters, and it is this API that will connect with the database, returning the results to you.

The REST API will be a service provider. You can even provide services publicly to anyone you want to consume.

An example of rest API to be consumed publicly can be found in the following URL:

developer.marvel.com

The REST architecture works on top of HTTP, so taking advantage of the checks that this protocol already performs natively.

A REST API is much faster to implement at the expense of the Simple Object Access Protocol (SOAP) API, and it's faster to run.

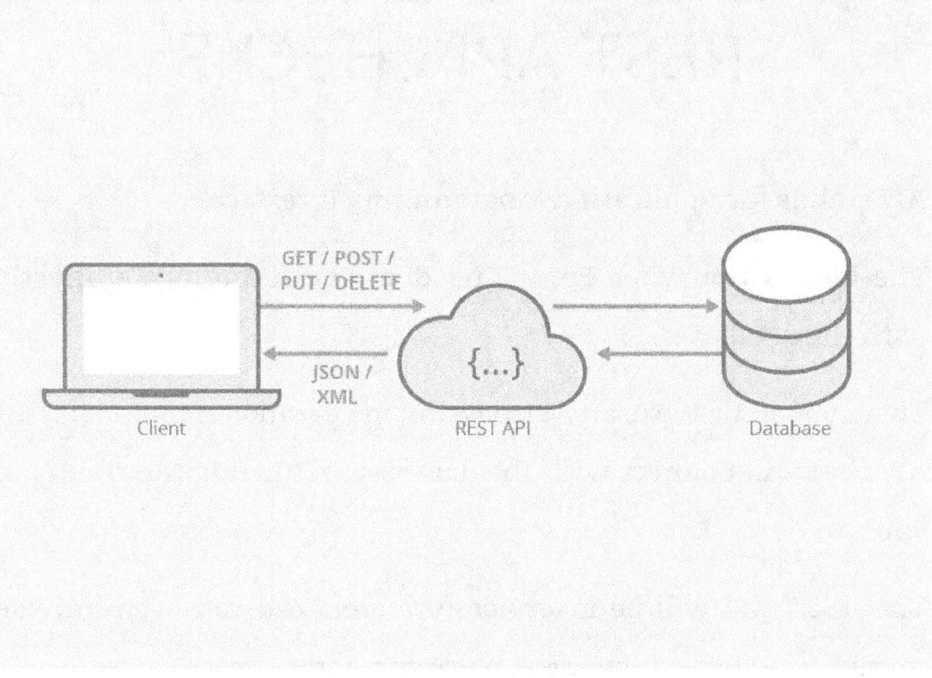

The api call structure is:

(Protocol)://(server:Port)/(context)/(resource)

The client will invoke some of the 4 main verbs (REST METHODS) for the API, and it will query the database, returning to the client the result in JSON or XML format.

The callback will also bring a STATUS CODE. They're well-known.

For example, 401 Forbidden, 404 Not Found, 500 Internal Server Error.

Sure. What about the tests of this API?

These tests can be used by the REST-ASSURED tool.

Just as we did with JUNIT earlier, we'll do with Rest Assured via Pom file.xml that builder Maven reads. Keep JUNIT and add Rest-Assured:

```
RestAssured/pom.xml

 1 <project xmlns="http://maven.apache.org/POM/4.0.0" xmlns:xsi
 2    <modelVersion>4.0.0</modelVersion>
 3    <groupId>apitest</groupId>
 4    <artifactId>RestAssured</artifactId>
 5    <version>0.0.1-SNAPSHOT</version>
 6    <dependencies>
 7      <dependency>
 8          <groupId>io.rest-assured</groupId>
 9          <artifactId>rest-assured</artifactId>
10          <version>4.3.0</version>
11          <scope>test</scope>
12      </dependency>
13      <dependency>
14          <groupId>io.rest-assured</groupId>
15          <artifactId>json-schema-validator</artifactId>
16          <version>4.3.0</version>
17      </dependency>
18      <dependency>
19          <groupId>io.rest-assured</groupId>
20          <artifactId>json-path</artifactId>
21          <version>4.3.0</version>
22      </dependency>
23      <dependency>
```

So you're ready to create the REST API tests.

The idea is very similar to what we did at JUNIT.

Go to src/test/java and create an APItest .java.

For example, let's say you want to test headers, response codes , and body.

We would have a written test similar to the following:

```java
package com.rest.test;

import static io.restassured.RestAssured.given;
import static org.hamcrest.CoreMatchers.equalTo;
import static org.hamcrest.Matchers.lessThan;
import org.testng.annotations.Test;
import io.restassured.RestAssured;

public class ValidateResponse {
    @Test
    public void getMethodCall() {
        RestAssured.baseURI = "https://req.in/api/users";

        given().queryParam("page", "2").header("Content-Type", "application/json").
        when().get().
        then().log().all()
                .assertThat().statusCode(200)
                .assertThat().time(lessThan(5000L))
                .assertThat().header("Content-Type", "application/json; charset=utf-8")
                        .header("Connection", "keep-alive")
                .assertThat().body("page", equalTo(2));
    }
}
```

As we've seen the tests at JUNIT, just look at the Rest Assured test and we've already identified assert and its goals.

The novelty is for the assertive **When** and **Then**.

Since in this book we do not seek to teach programmers how to create their tests but to teach DevSecOps and Pipeline with Jenkins, we will not delve into the topic.

The goal is to present how an API test is done, because just as the JUNIT result is consumed by SonarQube, so will the API tests.

The idea is the same, ensuring code coverage.

FUNCTIONAL TEST WITH SELENIUM

It is a more expensive test because it generates a lot of work to refactor the application and find where the root of the failure is.

The idea is to test user interactions with your application. We'll use the Selenium.

Selenium automates executions in the browser. I'll create navigations through the app.

Selenium uses a driver. Just go to google and search for a driver for your specific browser (and more, with the specific version).

For example, you can download directly from googleapis.com chromedriver version, in the version of your browser (if you are using Chrome).

After installing, you will add to path of system environment variables the path from which you launched your driver.

Next, we will change the Pom.XML Maven file in addition to JUNIT, now insert the Selenium.

```xml
<properties>
 <selenium.version>2.53.1</selenium.version>
 <testng.version>6.9.10</testng.version>
</properties>

<dependencies>
 <dependency>
  <groupId>org.seleniumhq.selenium</groupId>
  <artifactId>selenium-java</artifactId>
  <version>${selenium.version}</version>
 </dependency>
 <dependency>
  <groupId>org.testng</groupId>
  <artifactId>testng</artifactId>
  <version>${testng.version}</version>
  <scope>test</scope>
 </dependency>
</dependencies>
```

Next, we'll create the tests the same way we did junit and rest assured:

```java
import org.openqa.selenium.By;
import org.openqa.selenium.JavascriptExecutor;
import org.openqa.selenium.WebDriver;
import org.openqa.selenium.chrome.ChromeDriver;

public class Third {

    public static void main(String[] args) {

        // System Property for Chrome Driver
        System.setProperty("webdriver.chrome.driver", "D:\\ChromeDriver\\chromedriver.exe");

        // Instantiate a ChromeDriver class.
        WebDriver driver=new ChromeDriver();

        // Launch Website
        driver.navigate().to("http://www.javatpoint.com/");

        //Maximize the browser
        driver.manage().window().maximize();

        //Scroll down the webpage by 5000 pixels
        JavascriptExecutor js = (JavascriptExecutor)driver;
        js.executeScript("scrollBy(0, 5000)");

        // Click on the Search button
        driver.findElement(By.LinkText("Core Java")).click();
```

When the test is run, the driver will open your browser at the requested address, testing the application in this simple check above.

But the interesting thing about a functional test is not just testing if it's in the air. We need to test the simulation of the user interacting with the interface, clicking buttons, filling in fields.

For this we will do something like:

```java
driver.findElement(By.id("add")).click();
```

If I want to fill in a field, I'll use:

```java
driver.findElement(By.id("task")).sendKeys("Teste via Selenium")
```

I can even work with the returns, by summing the result into a local variable:

```
String message = driver.findElement(By.id("message")).getText()
Assert.assertEquals("Success!", message);
```

Note that we use JUNIT Assert to verify that the return

At the end, we will close the browser:

```
driver.quit();
```

SELENIUM GRID

To run WebDriver commands on remote machines, we will use the Selenium Grid.

It will balance the tests between the different platforms (Nodes).

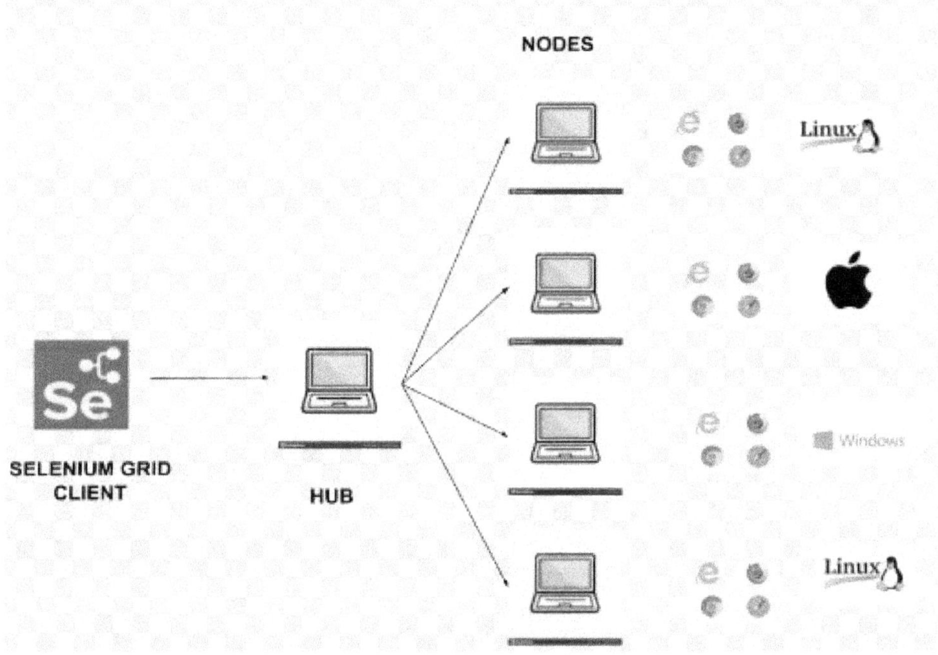

With Selenium Grid, the develop will no longer call the browser driver, but will use the DesiredCapabilities class.

```java
public class Grid   {
    WebDriver driver;
    String baseUrl, nodeURL;

    @BeforeTest
    public void setUp() throws MalformedURLException {
        baseUrl = "http://new.demo.com/";
        nodeURL = "http://192.168.1.4:566/hub";
        DesiredCapabilities capability = DesiredCapabilities.firefox();
        capability.setBrowserName("firefox");
        capability.setPlatform(Platform.XP);
        driver = new RemoteWebDriver(new URL(nodeURL), capability);
    }

    @AfterTest
    public void afterTest() {
        driver.quit();
    }

    @Test
    public void simpleTest() {
        driver.get(baseUrl);
        Assert.assertEquals("Welcome ", driver.getTitle());
    }
}
```

JENKINS PIPELINE - ANOTHER FORM OF INTEGRATION

Instead of creating the DevSecOps pipeline using jenkins' Freestyle option, we can seamlessly integrate using the Pipeline Plugin.

This plugin is often as plugins suggested by jenkins installation itself.

Basically, you'll follow the following steps in your Jenkins:

First, create a Jenkins item.

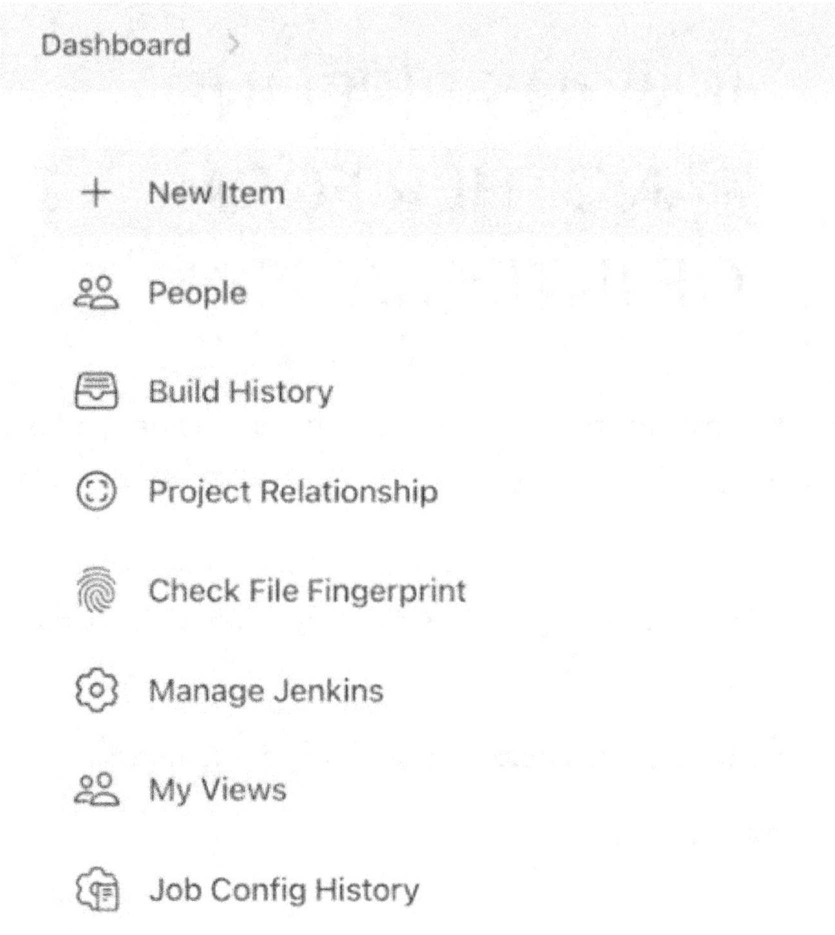

Dashboard >

+ New Item

People

Build History

Project Relationship

Check File Fingerprint

Manage Jenkins

My Views

Job Config History

Then select the Pipeline item:

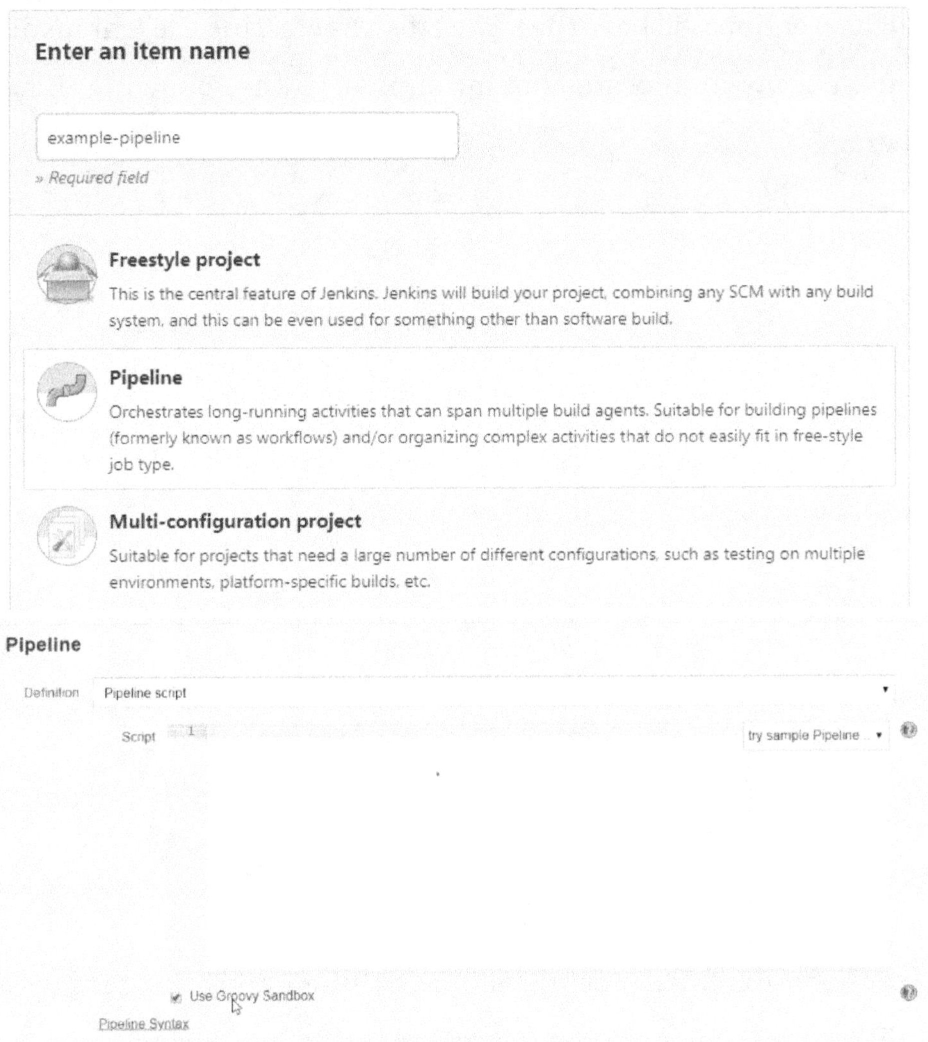

The script uses the Groovy language. It's very simple, it doesn't require prior knowledge.

You could do this by creating a file called Jenkinsfile. Are 2 forms, either using the graphical interface, or using the Jenkins file textfile.

Such an action will have the same effect as creating the Jenkinsfile, and you would allocate content similar to the following image there:

```
Jenkinsfile (Declarative Pipeline)
pipeline {
    agent any
    stages {
        stage('Stage 1') {
            steps {
                echo 'Hello world!'
            }
        }
    }
}
```

See that the created pipeline only has 1 stage, and at that stage we will send an echo (print on output) to the defined string.

In addition, we tell Jenkins to allocate an agent to this pipeline.

When you run this simple pipeline, you'll see in console output the following:

✓ Console Output

```
Started by user Jenkins
[Pipeline] Start of Pipeline
[Pipeline] node
Running on Jenkins in /Users/mac/.jenkins/workspace/example-pipeline
[Pipeline] {
[Pipeline] stage
[Pipeline] { (Stage 1)
[Pipeline] echo
Hello world!
[Pipeline] }
[Pipeline] // stage
[Pipeline] }
[Pipeline] // node
[Pipeline] End of Pipeline
Finished: SUCCESS
```

Ideally, you get used to always using creation via Jenkinsfile, because more complex projects will be unfeasible to manage through the graphical interface.

For a little while, Jenkins has a tool called Snippet Generator, which displays functions and generates skeletons for use in the script.

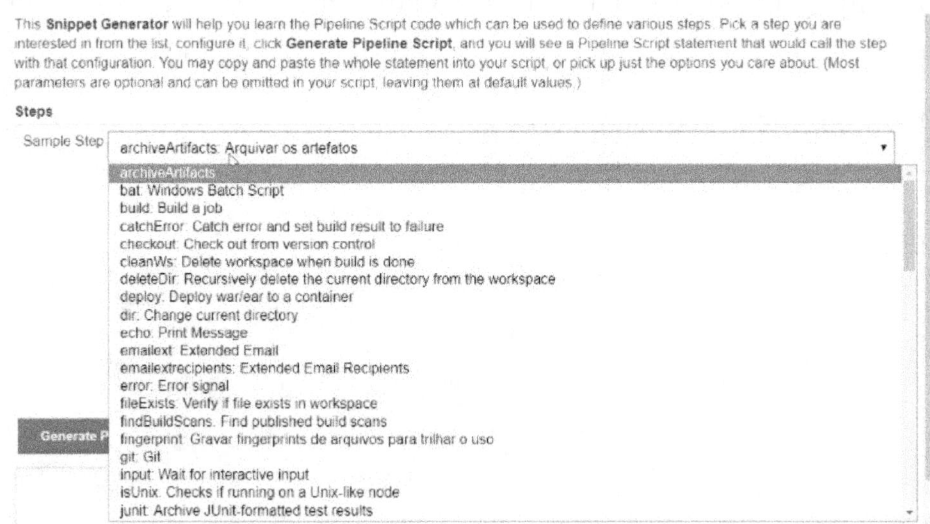

When you create via Jenkinsfile, you will not use the graphical interface script pipeline. You will select the option to search the SCM for your Jenkinsfile there on the Jenkins Pipeline screen that we saw earlier.

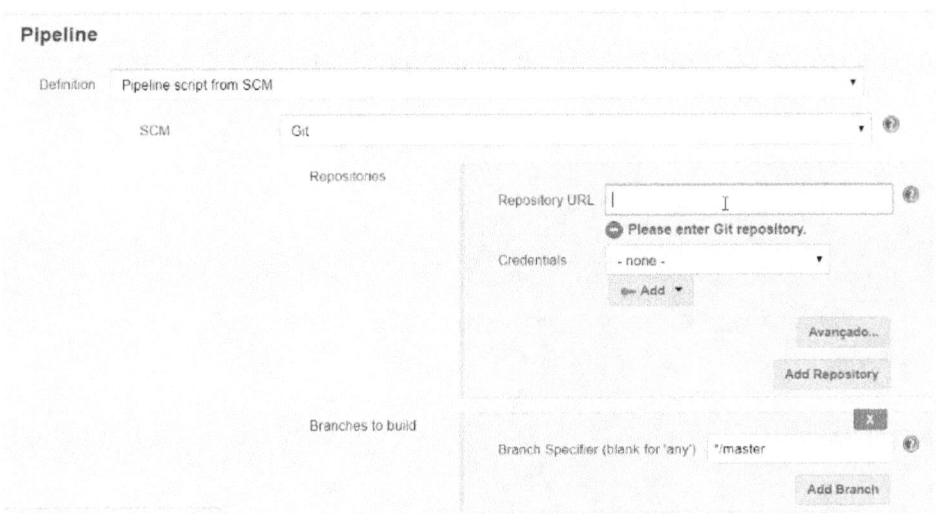

Configure credentials for access to your source code manager.

You will then have there in that your SCM (for example GIT), the Jenkinsfile file.

Important to know that it is case sensitive. Only the first letter of the Jenkinsfile file name is capitalized.

Script Path   Jenkinsfile

Lightweight checkout

Pipeline Syntax

Where there is Script Path above, understand that it is the relative path within your SCM where this Jenkinsfile file can be found.

In fact, if you have questions about the syntax to be used, Jenkins himself offers the link to the Snippet Generator page here , according to the image link: Pipeline Sintax.

An example of Jenkinsfile can be seen in the following image:

```
Jenkinsfile
 1 pipeline {
 2     agent any
 3     stages {
 4         stage ('Compile Stage') {
 5
 6             steps {
 7                 withMaven(maven : 'apache-maven-3.6.1') {
 8                     bat 'mvn clean compile'
 9                 }
10             }
11         }
12         stage ('Testing Stage') {
13
14             steps {
15                 withMaven(maven : 'apache-maven-3.6.1') {
16                     bat 'mvn test'
17                 }
18             }
19         }
20         stage ('Install Stage') {
21             steps {
22                 withMaven(maven : 'apache-maven-3.6.1') {
23                     bat 'mvn install'
24                 }
25             }
26         }
27     }
28 }
```

This Jenkinsfile defines a 3-stage pipeline.

In the first stage, the code is compiled using Maven.

Note that we have selected version 3.6.1 of Maven.

In addition, we use the BAT directive to execute a batch command, that is, the call to Maven with the clean and compile parameter.

In the second stage, we invoke unit tests. For this, we call Maven passing as a parameter the design of the tests with those test classes that we saw in the previous topics.

At the end, the last step performs the application deploy, calling the Maven with the install parameter.

Simple, isn't it?

Let's say our pipeline doesn't deploy, so we don't have the Maven install command to run.

In this case, after running the pipeline, we will have the following output in the Jenkins graphical interface:

Pipeline Pipeline

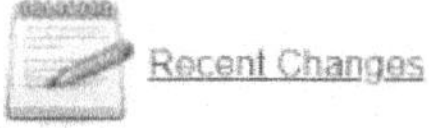

Stage View

	Declarative: Checkout SCM	Build	Unit Tests
Average stage times: (Average full run time: ~9s)	1s	4s	3s
#3 Mar 18 08:38 1 commit	1s	4s	3s
#2 Mar 18 08:35 1 commit	1s	4s	

That is, it displays the steps, and the time spent on each, including keeping history of the last executions.

ADDED STATIC ANALYSIS TO PIPELINE

Now that it's easy to understand how the pipeline works and maintains, let's then add one more step, which is the call to SonarQube for it to do static analysis of the code.

In fact, Jenkins will send him the data collected from the test pitch, and SonarQube will perform the calculations on top of that output, returning the notes.

First, let's go to Jenkins to locate the name we gave for our Sonar facility.

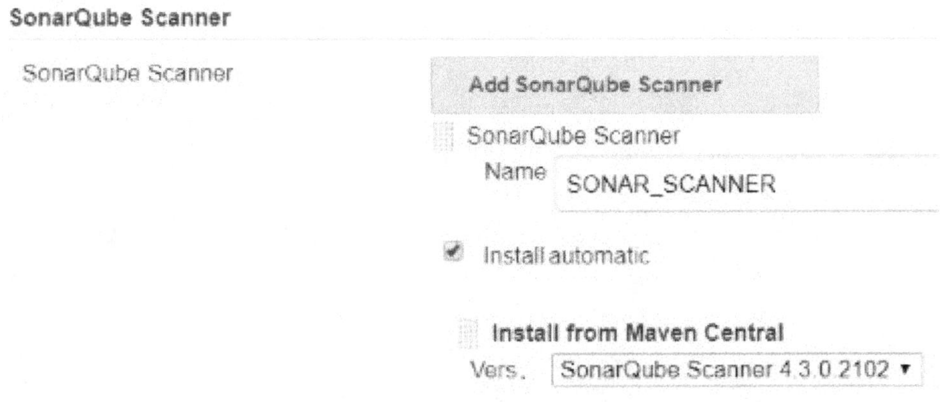

Next, we'll go to our Jenkinsfile adding the stage to Sonar:

```
stage ('Unit Tests') {
    steps {
        bat 'mvn test'
    }
}
stage ('Sonar Analysis') {
    environment {
        scannerHome = tool 'SONAR_SCANNER'
    }
```

See that first, I declare an environment variable that will be the link to the scanner that i picked up the name there on that previous screen. Use the tool directive.

Now, we add the step where we will call the scanner and pass the parameters to it.

To retrieve these parameters, I go there in jenkins' BUILD tab and retrieve the parameters that are passed to Sonar. They are in the Analysis Properties field. We've done that in previous chapters.

JDK	(Inherit From Job)
	JDK to be used for this SonarQube analysis
Path to project properties	
Analysis properties	sonar.projectKey=DeployBack sonar.host.url=http://localhost:9000 sonar.login=cf6826d57f1e453e08ecbd6cf86249647206f166 sonar.java.binaries=target sonar.coverage.exclusions="**/.mvn/**","**/src/test/**","**/model/**","**/Application.java"
Additional arguments	
JVM Options	

Now, we call the scanner passing these parameters.

Again, we have to add -D in front of each parameter.

```
        stage ('Unit Tests') {
            steps {
                bat 'mvn test'
            }
        }
        stage ('Sonar Analysis') {
            environment {
                scannerHome = tool 'SONAR_SCANNER'
            }
            steps {
                withSonarQubeEnv('SONAR_LOCAL') {
                    bat "${scannerHome}/bin/sonar-scanner -e -Dsonar.projectKey=DeployBack -Dsonar.host.url=http://
                }
            }
        }
    }
}
```

Okay, we now have the step for sonar analysis.

When running, Jenkins displays the new step.

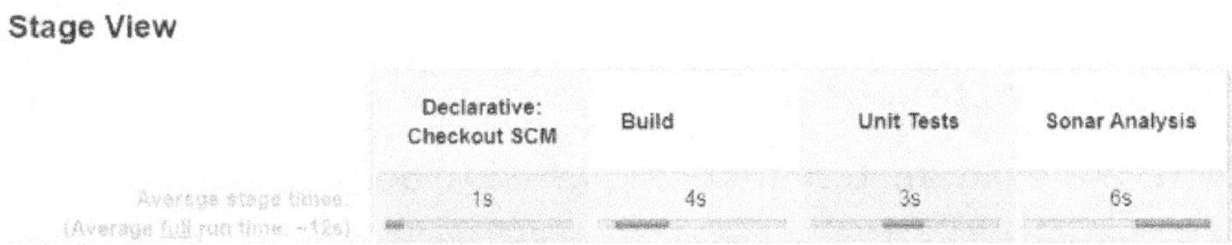

Stage View

	Declarative: Checkout SCM	Build	Unit Tests	Sonar Analysis
Average stage times. (Average full run time: ~12s)	1s	4s	3s	6s

ADDED QUALITY GATE STAGE

Now, let's add an internship to quality gate:

```
stage ('Quality Gate') {
    steps {
        timeout(time: 1, unit: 'MINUTES') {
            waitForQualityGate abortPipeline: true
        }
    }
}
```

This function will make a request to Quality Gate, asking if you have already completed your step.

You can add a Sleep (time) before the timeout to avoid overloading check calls.

So we have this new stage.

Stage View

	Declarative: Checkout SCM	Build	Unit Tests	Sonar Analysis	Quality Gate
Average stage times: (Average full run time: ~14s)	1s	3s	3s	5s	2s

ADDED DEPLOY STAGE

Now let's add the last stage, the deploy stage.

You will go into the graphical interface and use the Jenkins functionality to generate the script for you:

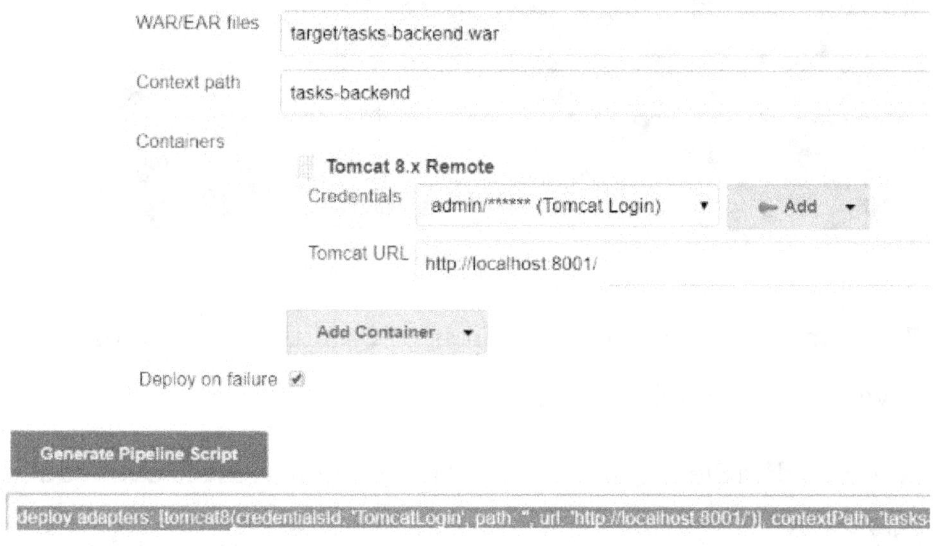

Now, just go to Jenkinsfile and create a Stage using this entire script:

```
stage ('Deploy Backend') {
    steps {
        deploy adapters: [tomcat8(credentialsId: 'TomcatLogin', path: '', url: 'http://localhost:8001/')],
    }
}
```

Again, running our Jenkins, the Deploy step will appear:

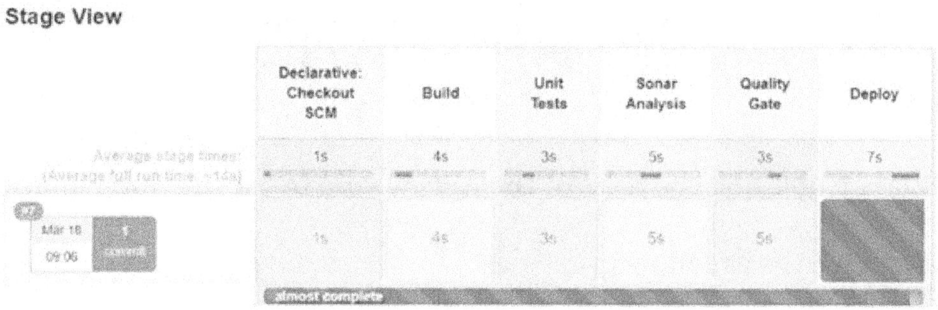

Stage View

	Declarative: Checkout SCM	Build	Unit Tests	Sonar Analysis	Quality Gate	Deploy
Average stage times: (Average full run time: ~14s)	1s	4s	3s	5s	3s	7s
Mar 18 09:06 current	1s	4s	3s	5s	5s	

almost complete

Important: When you run Jenkins, the Deploy step will only appear on the screen after the Quality Gate step if you have placed Sleep.

ADDING THE STAGE
TO API TESTS

We can also add the tests of the APIs we did in the previous topic.

They will be as follows:

```
stage ('API Test') {
    steps {
        dir('api-test') {
            git credentialsId: 'github_login', url: 'https://github.com/tasks-api-test'
            bat 'mvn test'
        }
    }
}
```

We have the DIR directive, where I'll select the directory where the step will be performed.

This step will play in the api-test directory

CREATING THE STAGE FOR FUNCTIONAL TESTS

You've learned what functional tests are and how you create them, now let's create the pipeline stage for them.

In fact, it is identical to the previous stage of API testing. The difference is only the url of the github where the tests will be downloaded.

It also differs by the DIR directive where we will now pass the directory for these functional tests.

```
stage ('Functional Test') {
    steps {
        dir('functional-test') {
            git credentialsId: 'github_login', url: 'https://github.com/tasks-functional-tests
            bat 'mvn test'
        }
    }
}
```

After execution, we have:

Stage View

	Declarative: Checkout SCM	Build	Unit Tests	Sonar Analysis	Quality Gate	Deploy	API Test	Functional Test
Average stage times (Average full run time: ~20s)	1s	4s	3s	5s	4s	6s	5s	9s

With this, we complete the Pipeline with all the steps.

See that to add new stages, just insert them into Jenkinsfile.

For example, if you want to deploy using docker, you would do something like:

```
stage('Deploy docker {
    steps {
            bat 'docker-compose build'
            bat 'docker-compose up -d'
    }
}
```

Of course, pre-configuring there in Docker your compose and other files needed for generating the image and allocating it in a Container.

In case you don't have this knowledge about Containers, at the end of this book there is a link to my book where I teach what Docker, Kubernetes and OpenShift are.

FINAL CONSIDERATIONS

With the knowledge gained in this book, you can change the culture of your software development by upgrading to DevSecOps standards.

If your company doesn't already use a DevSecOps pipeline, it will certainly adopt soon, so it's very interesting that you have that vision.

Even if you're a developer and not an infrastructure analyst, it's very important to know these fundamentals so that you can interact with the architecture team and propose changes to the pipeline to meet the needs of the development team.

BOOKS BY THIS AUTHOR

Kubernetes Containers In Openshift: For Beginners In Kubernetes

Container architecture is certainly the world's largest generator of remote jobs.

This book aims to teach the beginner what Docker is, and what Kubernetes is. It is the basis for any other platform on the market such as Amazon AWS, Microsoft Azure, and others.

After this setting, we will know all the power of RedHat OpenShift tools, which is a customized version of Kubernetes.

But even if you don't work with OpenShift in the end, you'll have mastered all of Kubernetes' core concepts like using Podman, and you'll have extreme ease of understanding any other platform.

We'll start with the general concepts, going through the command-line tools and end up enjoying the beautiful web interface that it presents for management.

If you don't know what Docker is and what Kubernetes is, the opportunity has come.

www.ingramcontent.com/pod-product-compliance
Lightning Source LLC
Chambersburg PA
CBHW061324120726

48001CB00002B/685